Published by Creative Education
123 South Broad Street, Mankato, Minnesota 56001
Creative Education is an imprint of The Creative Company

Design and production by Stephanie Blumenthal
Printed in the United States of America

Photographs by Jay Ireland & Georgienne Bradley, Eugene G. Schulz, Tom Stack & Associates (Erwin & Peggy Bauer,
Chip & Jill Eisenhart, Jeff Foott, Kitchin & Hurst, Joe McDonald, Greg Vaughn, Dave Watts)
Copyright © 2007 Creative Education

Library of Congress Cataloging-in-Publication Data

Bodden, Valerie.
Rainforests / by Valerie Bodden.
p. cm. — (Our world)
Includes index.
ISBN-13 : 978-1-58341-465-1
1. Rain forests—Juvenile literature. 2. Rain forest ecology—Juvenile literature. I. Title. II. Series.
QH86.B63 2006   578.734—dc22   2005053719

First Edition
2 4 6 8 9 7 5 3 1

OUR WORLD

R A I N F O R E S T S

Valerie Bodden

A rainforest is a kind of **forest**. Rainforests are found near the **equator** (ee-KWAY-ter). Most rainforests are very big. The biggest rainforest in the world is called the Amazon rainforest. Most of the Amazon rainforest is in a country called Brazil.

Rainforests are very hot. They are hot all year long. Rainforests are even hot in the winter! Rainforests get lots of rain. It rains most days in rainforests. The air in rainforests feels steamy!

Lots of animals live in hot rainforests

Rainforests have lots of trees. The trees grow close to each other. Some of the trees are short. Others are very tall. Rainforests have lots of flowers, too.

Some trees in rainforests have thick trunks

Rainforests are full of  animals. Some of the animals are big. Elephants live in some rainforests. So do hippos. Other animals in rainforests are small. Mice and  frogs are small. They live in rainforests, too.

There are many forms of life in rainforests

Lots of **insects** live in rainforests. Ants are insects. They live in rainforests. Butterflies are flying insects. They live in rainforests, too.

Many rainforest bugs have bright colors

Lots of birds fly through rainforests. Most of the birds have bright feathers. Some birds are blue. Others are green. Some are red. Some birds are lots of colors. The birds fill the air with their songs!

These rainforest birds are called parrots

Some animals live high in the trees of rainforests. They live in the **canopy**.  Monkeys and snakes live in the canopy. Lizards live in the canopy, too. Some of the animals in the canopy stay in the trees all the time. They never go down to the ground!

A rainforest's canopy is high above the ground

Some kinds of
animals live only
in rainforests

Many people are hurting rainforests. Some people cut down the trees in rainforests. They use the trees for wood. Other people cut down rainforests to make room for fields. Lots of plants and animals die when rainforests are cut down.

Some people work to keep rainforests safe. They stop people from cutting down trees. They want to save the plants and animals that live in rainforests!

Animals of all sizes need rainforests to live

Plants in rainforests grow toward the sun. You can make a plant grow toward the sun, too. Turn a potted plant on its side. Put it in a window. Water the plant when the dirt gets dry. Watch the plant. Does it grow sideways? Or does it grow up toward the sun?

GLOSSARY

canopy—the tops of the highest trees in rainforests

equator—the make-believe line between the top and bottom parts of Earth

forest—a place with lots of trees

insects—bugs that have six legs

LEARN MORE ABOUT RAINFORESTS

All About Rainforests
http://www.zoomschool.com/subjects/rainforest

Rainforest Heroes
http://www.rainforestheroes.com/kidscorner

Rainforest Alliance: Kids
http://www.rainforest-alliance.org/programs/education/kids/index.html

INDEX